Bruce C. Smeltz

HOWE LIBRARY
SHENANDOAH COLLEGE &
CONSERVATORY OF MUSIC
WINCHESTER, VA.

T5-BCL-616

Room for Error

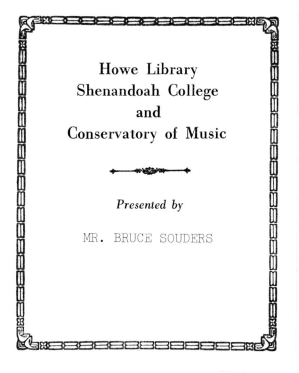

Howe Library
Shenandoah College
and
Conservatory of Music

Presented by

MR. BRUCE SOUDERS

HOWE LIBRARY
SHENANDOAH COLLEGE &
CONSERVATORY OF MUSIC
WINCHESTER, VA.

Room for Error

CHARLES MARTIN

Athens
The University of Georgia Press

Copyright © 1978 by the University of Georgia Press
Athens 30602

All rights reserved

Set in 10 on 12 point Monticello type
Printed in the United States of America

Library of Congress Cataloging in Publication Data

Martin, Charles, 1942–
    Room for error.
    I. Title.
PS3563.A72327R6   811'.5'4   77–6755
ISBN 0–8203–0425–5

PS
3563
.A72327
R6
1978
811 M363r

Martin, Charles

Room for error

0 7 6 ~ ~

For Leslie Martin

Acknowledgments

"Persistence of Ancestors," "Scenes Drawn from Life in Buffalo, New York," "November's Gate," "Four for Theodore Roethke," "Weekend (After Godard)," "Leaving Buffalo," "After," parts 1, 3, and 7 of "Institutional Life," "Heroic Attitudes," "Calvus in Ruins," "Sharks at the New York Aquarium," "Proposal for a Monument of Pears," and "Love in the City of Light Bent Back" first appeared in *Poetry*. Other poems were published in *Perspectives, New Generation: Poetry, The Centennial Review, Poetry Northwest*, and *Marilyn*.

Contents

IV

I

Persistence of Ancestors

1

The nineteenth century is not yet over
Here in Buffalo, at Forest Lawn;
A weeping, waning landscape seems to mirror
All of the treacheries of slow decline
That stop at nightfall: in the luny dark
This city of the dead amusement park

Still holds its own against the funeral
Parlors and the car lot's tacky smear
Of yellow neon, making its hard sell—
The nineteenth century won't disappear:
It bides its time, waiting out the age,
Each Robber Baron in his gilded cage. . . .

2

Red Jacket's graven prophecy still stands
Above the famous statue of the Chief:
"When I am gone and my warnings are no longer heeded,
The craft and avarice of the white man will prevail.
My heart fails me when I think of my people
So soon to be scattered and forgotten."

3

Almost too depressing now to bear,
The gross conjunction of vulgarity
And opulence the brokers planted here—

3

Art as the servant of Gentility,
The Bride of Commerce. Old Red Jacket waits.
The dead are gathered by the massy gates

Stolen from Europe, opening on Main
Street's traffic pouring in an endless flood
Past Williams' Paints, whose emblematic stain
Drips from the Arctic like a flow of blood,
Or like a great red tongue, ambiguously curled
Above its motto: "Covering The World."

November's Gate

My paradise, my urban pastoral
Of isolated buildings which surround
An empty ballfield: tunnels underground
Link up the buildings, echo when we call!
Like children in an attic, we explore
Abandoned rooms, each other, we try on
Old-fashioned fashions, wrap each other up in
Bedsheets used to cover furniture . . .
No characters, no action: at midnight a mirror
Wobbles on its pivots. Up on tip-toes
You tilt it downward, and your image spills
Like quicksilver over the wooden dresser—
Tilted back up, it patiently refills.
When we go out at last, it overflows.

5

Scenes Drawn from Life in Buffalo, New York

1

Barbaric children occupy the grand
Old houses that the brokers lived in once.
They fornicate in growing disrepair,
They paint themselves for feasts, they smoke and dance,
The fresh blood caking in their matted hair. . . .
The brokers wait. They cannot understand.

2

The politicians settle up old scores:
The city trembles, its foundations shake.
Puppets move their lips, endlessly clever,
Skilled at faultless mimicry: they make
Important points. And when each speech is over,
Standing ovations cover running sores.

3

Vanilla ice cream in unmelting splendor,
The Blocher Family Memorial
At Forest Lawn. The Blocher family
Celebrates its endless funeral,
Proving to visitors that death can be
An acquisition, rather than surrender.

4

Between nostalgia and anticipation,
Midsummer fever and midwinter snow,
The city takes its after-dinner nap:
The Home Edition of *The Buffalo*
Evening News goes skidding from its lap
Like a small avalanche of self congratulation.

Satyr, Cunnilinguent: To Herman Melville

1

Winding her fingers through
His hair, warmly drumming
Her fingertips, leading him to
The sharp verge of her coming,

Her passion at its flood
Overwhelms all measure;
On articulation's bud,
Inarticulate with pleasure,

She flops like a caught fish,
Straining to be human!
This Satyr has his wish
Fulfilled in a mortal woman.

2

Flesh cancels mystery:
Had Billy a young bride
As Ahab had, would he
Not have been less tongue-tied?

Might he not have been
Glib in the face of darkness?
—As you yourself, in
Some moods seem to practice

The clever, tongue-in-cheek
Art of the cunning Satyr.
How hard it is to speak
Of the things that matter.

During a Winter of Recurring Storms

Elaborate frail webs of ice were spun
Over the trees as soon as it was dark:
God the Spider's brilliant handiwork
Cracking and melting in the winter sun's

Thin gilt, extravagantly minimal.
We read through rows of ragged paperbacks
Underneath a print of Edward Hicks'
"Peaceable Kingdom." His whimsical

Beasts regarded us regarding them.
Stared at and stared at, they would turn their strange
Masks into faces and then quickly change
Back again to Lion, Leopard, Lamb.

9

Sunday in Delaware Park

Bobbing like apples in their tight
Skins of primary color, all in place,
Wound in unshadowed dreams of appetite
Before the beginning of the first race

In the Model Speedboat Competition—
A fleet of polished wooden shoes:
"Classics," we overhear, and "Lilliputian
Bombs, just waiting for the fuse. . . ."

At the lake's edge, mechanic hobbyists
Labor to put each darling through its paces—
Middle-aged suburban terrorists
Manqué—crew-cut, with the ascetic faces

Of men who tortured animals as boys.
Denied their fatal choices in the name
Of something better, they trot out their toys,
Driving in like outlaws from the tame

Provinces on Sunday to cut loose—
They bring their seething engines to a boil
Out of the water, lovingly they goose
The tiny hidden parts with drops of oil,

Then send them into action: off from shore
As though by instinct, deaf and blind,
Driven by short-wave radio, they lunge out for
The other side, the jugular: they bend

The surface under them and nearly spill,
Turning—but wind out straight to churn the lake's
Skin senseless as they slap and flail,
Mad with the terror of their tiny wakes—

We lean together toward the waiting shock
Of that conclusion into which they strain—
Abandoned houses waiting for the rock
That will shatter the last whole window pane—

But one by one they stutter and run dry
On impetus—for a moment they hover
Weightless, then skid down on the suddenly
Softening water and the race is over.

SIGNS

THIS PARK IS PUBLIC PROPERTY AND SHOULD
NOT WILL NOT CANNOT PLEASE OBEY
THE TREES WHOSE BRANCHES FLOURISH AS YOU WOULD
SCHOOLCHILDREN ON A TRIP OR HOLIDAY

BECAUSE OF ON THE LAWNS IS NOT ALLOWED
AND WILL BE VIOLATED BY THE TREES
GROWING IN SECTIONS WHERE THE NEWLY PLOWED
ARE NOT PERMITTED THEREFORE THEREFORE "PLEASE"

CURB YOUR SOFTBALL IS RESTRICTED TO
DESIGNATED AREAS THE ROSES
EXPOSING THEMSELVES TO THOSE "JUST PASSING THROUGH"
WILL ALL BE PUNISHED AFTER THIS PARK CLOSES

PLEASE REMEMBER ITS FOR OTHERS TOO
BEFORE YOU LEAVE FOR HOME PLEASE PICK UP ALL
SLEDDING BIKING JOGGING WATCHING YOU
DAILY AT FIVE WEEKENDS AT NIGHTFALL

Sonnet after Dante Alleghieri & Robert Duncan

Dreaming of an end to discontent
I often wish that you and I might be
Taken up, as though by sorcery
Through walls which offer no impediment
To Duncan's splendid craft, which had been sent
For us, for our circle, so that we
Might sail forever on that inner sea,
Spending our time where time is never spent.

But would we be content to live the way
That Duncan, after Dante, so approves?
Or find such joys impossible to bear,
Invent a thousand reasons not to stay·
Where we would find it hard to be ourselves,
Being so far removed from what we were.

Terminal Colloquy

O where will you go when the blinding flash
Scatters the seed of a million suns?
And what will you do in the rain of ash?

I'll draw the blinds and pull down the sash,
And hide from the light of so many noons.
But how will it be when the blinding flash

Disturbs your body's close-knit mesh,
Bringing to light your lovely bones?
What will you wear in the rain of ash?

I will go bare without my flesh,
My vertebrae will click like stones.
Ah. But where will you dance when the blinding flash

Settles the city in a holy hush?
I will dance alone among the ruins.
Ah. And what will you say to the rain of ash?

I will be charming. My subtle speech
Will weave close turns and counter turns —
No. What will you say to the rain of ash?
Nothing, after the blinding flash.

14

A Chair Ought to Stand on Its Own Two Legs,
Or,
The Art of Milton Avery

"Whatever is beautiful is tainted
(Whatever I paint for you can't be spoken,

Whatever I say to you can't be painted);
Whatever is genuine is broken."

Four for Theodore Roethke

I: *The Circle*

Out of the matrix of all metaphor
Resemblance came: one feather was a wing,
One wing a bird, circling before
The shaded absences of everything.
And when all birds were flown, his mind could seize
On the vibrating emptiness of trees,

Could make a song of what was almost there,
Tilting into what was nearly gone.
He loved the edges, where the changes are;
In a still place, he clattered like a stone
On the far side of things; the mirror's kiss,
A mountain nibbled on by its abyss,

The silence that surrounded every word,
Sheathlike, flamelike, quivering to sound—
It was in darkness he most clearly heard
The smallest cry out of the brewing ground,
The meanest voice, cracking like a whip.
He measured out the snail's becoming step,

Danced with bears, edged toward openings;
Standing at the center of his field
He brought us news of all insensible things,
The near, deep lives of another world:
Nudged by beginnings, echoes drew him out;
Inevitable endings cut him short.

II: *The Garden*

In the ruined kingdom of his father's house
There were no secrets, all the outside
Leaned like a lover on its fragile glass;
A bridegroom pressing a resistant bride
Would not lean heavier. He held his breath
And counted slowly; after ten came death.

But in the canceled greenhouse of his memory
When it was summer throughout all the year,
The vast, unmeasured outside let him be,
And even death backed down, speechless before
The iron mandate of his father's will.
He came back often to that citadel

Which looked to him as to an only child,
And stood in the fierce lightnings of his father's eye,
In the beauty and horror of a world
Where flowers tumbled from an old man's thigh,
All falling into light at his command—
In the upraised province of his father's hand

He cast no stones: waited, biding time;
Beyond the narrow garden was a field
And in that field the shadow of a rhyme
Fell across occasions which revealed
A world of endless, varied sequence; he
Bent to it, like a lover, secretly.

III: *The Dance*

All history was troubled by a dream,
The constant world shook with metaphor.
In an open field once before their time
He summoned her as water, aether, air—
Wishing was having then, and branch was root—
They flourished like the dead do, underfoot

(The dead have no perspective on events),
They came together there, they broke apart,
Were fiery as grass beneath a lens
And like the fishes in the water, wet.
He knew her body's risk, his body's task;
Wild speech took shape behind a formal mask,

Passion was measured in a patterned dance,
A dance the dead do, all out of place
(The easy dead are anywhere at once);
He taught her words she knew, and he learned grace.
Each hung in silence on the other's lips:
Dead children quivered at their fingertips,

Rippling like rumors through a long embrace,
Or bent back steeply like a candle flame
To feed in whispers on an empty face—
In that fond dancing each of them became
The other's answer to the asking dead.
—How one would follow where the other led!

IV: *The Burden*

The burden flowering at heavy cost:
He knew the cost, knew how the burgeoning
Bough shudders in the wind, already lost—
And the heavy price paid when the opening
Buds become the blossoms on a tree;
Those blossoms ripen and they break their bough.

No longer pacing out his middle age,
He tumbled quickly to an ecstacy,
He loosened into love, that purest rage,
Impossible to risk or justify:
Circumference was never more than here
And now, no end was on it, anywhere—

There was no edge, there was no edge at all!
He knew the virtue of some secret name,
It was impossible for him to fall:
Bobbing like a blossom on a stem
He was indifferent to all but joy,
And with his words he gave himself away:

Inside the cherry is the lightest stone,
But nonetheless the cherry's branches cry
Out at its weight: they cannot bear for long
The burden of their joy. No more could he.
That heavy body bore a glistening word.
Now fold his hands away, misunderstood.

Weekend (After Godard)

"Erotic cannibals, we eat up
Everyone, each other: is *gourmandise*
A verb? Stripping me for form's sake with his eyes,
One index finger stirred a paper cup
Half-full of ice and scotch, we heard the Stones
Make plastic revolution . . . I was bored
With him, with having him as my reward
For clean living: I wanted beads and bones,
Necklaces of chipped teeth. . . .
                            Those nights at your
Place in the Village. I thought of our
One-room fortress falling. History
Is what goes on in spite of us, outside—
Warpainted Mohawks with machine guns glide
By noiselessly, slip from tree to tree. . . ."

The Rest of the Robber Barons

1

Opening up one's dog-eared Tennyson
Or battered Arnold, one is led to dream
Of barren beaches, of a flamboyant, blood-red sun
Smeared messily against an asphalt sky
Beneath which no one picnics: all is all in doubt,
One follows the tide with one's eyes. The tide is History,
Or Culture, and it's clearly going out.
One follows the tide. One essays a scream.

2

The Dutch Elms holding sway at Forest Lawn
Regard the shrunken mansions of the Great,
The menopausal Nymph and sagging Faun
Now bickering among the marble slabs
And lachrymose Angels the Robber Barons gathered
When all of Europe was still up for grabs—
Bargains strewn here like the pillage scattered
By a losing army on a long retreat.

3

Safe in their vaults of Tiffany stained glass
And Carrara marble, the Robber Barons lie
Dreaming of railroads, dreaming of natural gas.
They grow more and more anonymous each season,
Each season a little less anxious to escape.
Yet even now, the souls of the Robber Barons listen
For Resurrection's clacking ticker tape
And the dead, rising like stocks, triumphantly.

Contractions

The universe converges. Continents
Drift toward each other like abandoned ships,
Rudderless, begging for conclusion—
On their frayed edges, I see people waving.
At Forest Lawn the grave stones rasp across
Their quaking coffin lids. Everyone is under
Arrest in Buffalo: the stern police
Move from street to street, question to question.
The evidence that will convict us all
Drifts in like snow and piles up everywhere.
At the other end of Delaware Avenue
Lake Erie shrivels like a severed hand.
Each empty bottle holds its scribbled note.
They litter the shore, sucking air like fish.

Leaving Buffalo

1

Others, many others, must have known
That it was waiting for them at the center—
It was the weather. The weather made it certain:
At winter's core, wished on by the sun,

A revelation waited to occur.
Those optimists! They took as their bright text,
"If not this year, why—certainly—the next!"
They felt that waiting built strong character.

2

Season after season brought new dread,
For it was dreadful to be always waiting,
Enduring what they knew was past debating.
"Be patient as spiders," their old people said.

"Our lives went wrong," their old people thought:
"But speak of Progress, how it all gets better,
And when it doesn't, how it doesn't matter.
Why should we tell them it was all for nought,

When what will last of us are our manners?"
They called abhorrent what was merely lewd,
But dreamt of applebreasted women: nude,
Bronze-skinned lovelies of the far savannas. . . .

3

"One leaves when it is easier to leave,
Knowing what one knows." So I hear some say.
Expecting nothing, I will leave today.
Others are waiting still and still believe

That it will happen soon, that they were chosen
To be there when it happened, when the wind
Must search the streets for living trees to bend
Under its steep breath, until their frozen

Hearts crack and all the shivered houses show
What we have always known was waiting there,
The hidden dream of fire everywhere
Flowering along each wooden row—

It hasn't happened yet. And yet it might.
On nights like this in autumn we pretend
That it will happen. All good things must end.
They glow inside their narrow shells tonight,

They rattle like dry peppercorns, the dead.
The leafless branches of the blighted Dutch
Elms they left as decoration touch
Awkwardly in the darkness overhead.

After

"Nothing happened after. For three days
We waited at the cottage by the lake.
John drove off to town one night for news
And didn't return. I led the children back
Into the woods. I said he'd meet us there.
Worn out too easily, both boys slept
So deeply that I searched their skin and hair. . . .
Later, I heard men calling, so I crept
Forward to the cottage . . . sheets of flame
Lay at the window and the open door,
Devouring our summer lives and goods.
I brought the boys back deeper in the woods
And told them we would look next morning for
A new summer place. I said it was a game."

II

Institutional Life

> "Poseidon sat at his desk doing figures. The
> administration of the waters gave him endless work."
> Kafka

1

Doctor, I dream that I am lost and mocked
By hidden voices calling out my name
Behind the doors of houses all the same,
And every door I try is always locked
But one: I open it and walk into
A room in which the hopeless mad are kept. . . .
Here no one speaks to me at all, except
For one shy girl who sees that I am new.
"There is a room beyond this one," she says.
"This one is called The Tank, and that's The Pen.
The guards are called The Angels of The Law.
In this room you may do just as you please,
But those who leave here don't come back again."
And then I wake up wondering what I saw.

2

"Penelope, Telemachos: both gone,
Translated into fiction—you survive,
Barely. If you want to stay alive
You've got to be as quiet as a stone.
This dresser's yours, this is your army cot.
Lunch this afternoon will be fish stew.
They'd want to kill you if they only knew,
They'd want to give you what the others got.
Don't tell them anything."
                                    And then she leaves.
Is she the daughter that I never had,
Or the Goddess, always counseling deceit?

I put on one more mask, one more defeat,
A nameless man going slowly mad.
Is it doing, or remembering deceives?

3

She slips beside me, takes an empty seat,
And smoothes a scrap of paper in her hands:
"Can you make out the writing?" she demands.
The page is blank. She reads me part of it:
"'Beaten by police,' his last notes say,
'For three days running. She would not confess.
M's understanding of the Camps grows less
And less improbable to me each day.
Most likely I will be the next to go;
Begun by chance, it ends of necessity. . . .'
That's very old, you know. What's written there.
I took it from a guard who slept with me.
He was tall and slim and had blond hair."
Why are you back, I ask her.
                              "Don't you know?"

4

"Believe it but be silent is the way.
Of course you don't remember—it will all
Come slowly back to you: first learn to crawl,
Then learn to walk. Remember that today

Could be the first day of your old, real life.
We must go slowly. There are others who
Are in on it—I've passed the word down through
A friendly guard who knew your son and wife.
In the next few days, a few of us will start
Speaking of it to a few we trust.
We must move slowly, for the walls have ears
And all the ears have walls. It might take years,
It might not happen ever, but we must
Live our lives as though it will: take heart."

5

The old connections break, old faces blur,
The greasy skin on a bowl of cold soup. . . .
Time's tripped me up, Time's caught me in a loop,
My daily matter. When I think of her
I think of no one: when I think of him,
I see the child I think I used to be;
We renovate the old gags easily,
By switching the direction of the film—
Flapping like wings the dated pages fly
Swarming back onto their calendar;
The custard plastered on the comic's face
Peels off and hurtles backward through the air,
Becoming, instantly, the hefted pie:
Always the audience is pleased by this.

6

"Returns to find men taking liberties:
The suitors in his place hand him a cup
Of wine, some meat. The suitors have made up
Stories of how King Odysseus
Returns to find men taking liberties,
The suitors in his place. Gladly they tell
How King Odysseus sent them to hell!
They tell him that a guest should wish to please,
They say, 'It's a wise beggar entertains.'
He rises slowly, winish, tottering:
Telling his story would be suicide.
He makes up an excuse and steps outside.
Begins to run. At his back the devouring
Legend follows, anxious for remains. . . ."

7

Every night we heard their senseless cries
Rise up and mingle in the hot air—
The wall between us sagged, dripping with their
Sweat, or billowed out to ecstacies,
Aching like a membrane, paper thin—
Her double, her double's foreign lover, who
Lay in there so closely that they knew
The walls around them as their only skin. . . .
They beat like moths against the one wall they
Shared with us, it was another world—
We listened for them, nights. Dying, they broke
Open like bread, their fractioned bodies spoke,

While we lay apart and tightly curled
In the damp palm of what we could not say.

8

All things are possible: the man I was
Or may have been was many men besides
And many beasts, all chained up as the tides
Are, all fiercely roaring as the wind does.
That was what the goddess Kirke knew,
My witching pedagogue. She taught me well:
"What follows function?"
                              "Form does."
                                          "That's the spell:
Each of your crewmen was a human zoo."
Embrace a goddess, penetrate her charms:
Simple as that. I might have gone to bed
With Kirke, studied magic in her arms:
"So many murders, armed robberies and rapes—
Your men *were* swine," Kirke might have said.
"Little labor, finding their true shapes."

9

He had no stories, feeding on the raw
Meat of experience, then voiding it:
The past was excrement to his small wit,
The future flesh to cram into his maw.

He narrowed my few options down to one:
"A good wine, but it doesn't travel well. . . ."
We left Poseidon's pinhead in his cell
Snoring and bubbling: he'd had his fun
And we'd had ours. Each night in his dreams
I am the clumsy self-pitying child,
He is the hero who can never lose.
And for an instant in his sleep we fuse
Together, one, before he leaps up wild
With pain, the steep cave cracking to his screams.

10

Assurances accept me: I fit in,
I take a part in things for my own good:
Last week I carved some figures out of wood.
All I have to do is toe the line
And keep my eye out for the basic flaw:
It's easy time. I almost like the life.
The other day I made myself a knife
Out of scraps, today I used the power saw. . . .
I see my enemies, their faces turn
Into the masks of bats flying to hell,
Slaughtered for their indolence and greed!
They tell me, "Work, keep busy, you'll get well. . . ."
I'm older now and slower—what I need
To know takes me much longer now to learn.

11

My name, repeated: her insistent shout
Is shattered by long laughter in the trees.
In my dream I mumble Dear God please
Let her find me this time let her lead me out.
Doctor, I've had this dream now for a week,
Always the same wilderness, the same
Long laughter shattering the shouted name.
She calls and calls me but I cannot speak.
What maid is this who does not fear the lion's
Eye and tangled mane and nakedness?
What god or goddess urges her to bring
Him from the bleak shore of that wilderness
To the city of her father, the mild king
Of the blameless and essential Phaiakians?

12

Her disappearance: elegant, almost
Flamboyant: grand! She's on the outside now,
I'm sure of it although I'm not sure how.
Vanished just like Hamlet's father's ghost . . .
The guards all tell me that she was removed:
"A troublemaker, not at all like you;
It wasn't nice, but what else could we do?
We asked permission and Himself approved."
I think this alters my uncertain role;
Maybe it's time for me to disappear,
Maybe I'll do it now.
                              This afternoon.

Tonight.
        I'll vanish down my rabbit hole
And then come back to haunt them:
                        KNOCK KNOCK
                                        "Who's there?"
A secret smile before I answer, "No one."

Mandrake Gestures Hypnotically

Devoured by images of appetite,
The Prince, enchanted, sucks an orange rind:
His eyes are shiny silver buttons that
Do not waver as the sharp teeth grind

Finely and precisely until they strip
From underneath the labored floppy skin
The last tenacious remnants of raw pulp.
He is content, he rubs his bearded chin

With one small fist before he lets his prize
Fall among scraps of grape and tangerine.
And now he's serious: the wide, bright eyes
Stare at something distant, foreign, green.

The Panther of Rainer Maria Rilke

Wearied with looking out, when all he knows
Are polished iron bars, multiplied
Into infinity, unyielding rows—
He feels as though there were no outside

At all, nothing but a circling around
A core of adamant, a nucleus—
As dancing bands of energy surround
A great will, inert and powerless.

The iris opens: an image glides through
Silently and moves beyond the eyes,
Down along the quivering muscles to
Enter the deep heart. And there it dies.

Heroic Attitudes

I

He has always feared the awakening dead,
Has offered his flesh to feed their hunger
When they rose in the darkness around his bed.
He has always feared their lordly anger.

This was their song: "An endless river,
Flowing in silence, carries us on
Through every weather. The past is the lover
You hold in your arms, going and gone."

He remembers the painful death of his father,
And often at night remembers the son
Set out to die in terrible weather.
His horse stumbles on a sharp stone.

He cannot escape to a different weather,
A place out of reach of the lordly dead.
Every night he must watch them gather
In a bright ring around his bed.

Today he rides through a distant wood
To answer a question or question an answer
Which once he thought he understood.
The black trees sway with the weight of their branches.

His wife, the Queen, turns from her mirror:
Below, in the courtyard, a riderless horse
Gallops in circles, plunging with terror,
Returned from where the three roads cross.

II

His wife, the Queen, turns from her mirror
The wind in the forest is combing its leaves
She combs her hair, which tumbles like fire
The wind in the forest quietly weaves
A chamber of silence over the King
Until his life is no more than a rumor
Covered by leaves that are withering
The lips of the King are twisting, not terror

Presses his mouth, not the mouth of a lover
But some indescribably slower thing
Winds through him like a meandering river
The plains of his flesh are rippling
When the rippling stops he will turn into stone
And the leaves will press dry fingers over
Lamentation of flesh, sorrow of bone
She sees it as in a dream, in a fever

And cries out aloud, shaking with terror
And the birds rise screaming and are gone
All taking flight from a single tremor
They have left her there in the forest alone
She combs out her hair in the forest a tree
Combs out its leaves, which tumble like fire
Burning to ashes her husband's body
And she sits in silence before her mirror

III

He wonders now, if, having so far defied
Whatever it was that told him clearly, "No!"
He may leave his sleeping, ambiguous bride;
Or, if he chooses instead not to go,

Will he be forced later to put on
A foolish mask, pretending ignorance
Of what he is and what it is he has done?
And while assorted figures do their dance

Of discovery, dredge up forgotten clues,
Come in with the truth wriggling on their hooks,
Must he pretend amazement at the maze?
—Guessing by their careless, smirking looks

That they have always known what now appears,
Monstrous, cold, slimy with afterbirth. . . .
Might he perhaps live on, unknown for years,
Until all who know are folded in the earth?

There is still time to leave before she wakes,
Rolling from sleep unsated, full of lust—
Pull down the shades, muffle all the clocks,
Slip out at dawn like her true husband's ghost—

There is no way to leave before her death,
For where would he go, and how could he be free?
The prize he won is ashes in his mouth,
But life here has a pleasing symmetry.

III

Calvus in Ruins

I

verbosa gaudet Venus loquella

Venus loves nothing more than juicy gossip,
lewd & lascivious badinage, highly
spiced with erotic words whose double meanings
      have double meanings:
that is what pleases her. and when she gets it,
swiftly her tongue insinuates its clever
tip into pauses in the conversation,
      exciting Rumor,
who flutters off in eighty-two directions
spreading all sorts of havoc   *   *
*   *   *   *   *   *
      even great cities.
therefore be careful if you have a secret
lover with whom you make love in great peril
of discovery: those sweet times are precious
      which you have stolen,
and only silence will allow you hours
more of such riches: words will never buy them,
words will only bring that mischief which Venus
      loves nothing more than.

II

*   *   *   *   *   my
delicate songs are popular at parties,
my   *   *   *   *   *
      have been collected;
yet he is certainly to be more envied
who may embrace you whenever he wishes,

even while I must lurk under your window,
     suffering bitter-
ly from chills & debilitating fevers,
which take their turns at racking my small body
until I stagger off in utter torment,
     mocked by *ragazzi!*
but these are trifles, which I mention only
to make this song of mine for your amusement
*   *   *   *   *   *
     if you would have me
while I am still sufficient to those pleasures
we shared together, when, in someone else's
*   *   *   *   *   *
     send me a few words.

III

*   *   *   *   *   *
*   *   *   *   *   *
*   *   *   *   *   *
     Caesar & Pompey:
one word from either, and whole armies perish
*   *   *   *   *   *
provinces catch fire, distant   *   *
     illuminated;
*   *   *   *   *   *
but what I've written will endure forever,
*   *   *   *   *   *
     strewn with blank corpses

46

IV

Whatever is likeliest to happen, does:
the maiden in the orchard is deflowered;
the drunken husband, home from brothel-hopping,
    finds his wife in bed
with Caesar & a few of Caesar's cronies;
some sickening old fool is given poison
by his young wife, unfettered as the weary
    day turns into night;
the marble children Praxiteles sired,
dismembered limb by limb, are *   *
*   *   parchment flares at the edges,
    then bursts into flame!
but in the distant provinces, decaying
corpses get up & trundle off to market
places already agog with the rumor
    of yet another
two-headed chicken, another virgin birth.
there, it would seem, all seeing is deceiving;
nothing is said that doesn't find believers;
    they fancy poets.

V

        (a)

Withering laurel: in his old age, Caesar
will have forgotten all of the costly gains
on British battlefields, in Roman bedrooms;
    sieges & conquests
which are now brilliant in his eyes will perish

      *   *   *   *   *   *
these ruined cities or those ruined women,
     equally nameless.
soon no one living will remember Caesar,
but memory itself will be forgotten
before your name is   *   *   *
     your slightest gesture;
*   *   *   *   *   *
*   *   like the crumbs of flowers
on a madman's chin   *   *   *
     *   *   *

      (b)

memory draws my bowstring, and the arrow
trembles a moment   *   *   *
*   *   *   indifferent to fame
     as any poet!

VI

a virgo infelix, herbis pasceris amaris

*   *   *   *   *   *
*   *   *   *   *   *
boredom's a bitter stalk for you to nibble,
     unlucky virgin;
outside the city everything is boring,
life is a nuisance   *   *   *
and Venus is indeed the most important
     goddess in heaven;
I'm sympathetic, I agree completely;

48

but even the sun that journeys endlessly
has sense enough to rest when near exhaustion:
    can't you do likewise?

VII

    (a)

Before your restless ashes had been sifted
the quick connective tissue of your poems
already had begun a slower burning;
    now next to nothing,
what little bits of you were spared for reading
hardly make sense—the dreck that critics salvaged
simply to score a point or two on usage,

    *   *   *

    (b)

once my rhetoric defeated Cicero's,
my eloquence made Vatinius sputter,
"must I be hanged because this shrimp can whistle?"
    that doesn't matter:
whatever we have made well will at last come
to utter nothing in the house of Orcus,

*   *   *   *   *   *
    *   *   *

49

VIII

Think of Achilles, maddened by his hatred,
leaping from one wet stone onto another,
pursuing those who are already shadows
    as he heads upstream,
an unrelenting fury in that river
where the cold-eyed fish tumbled in its currents
are delicately stripping bloated corpses
    of their fat cargo;
or think of women delicately weaving
patterns as subtle as the webs of spiders
*   *   *   *   *   *
    stained with human blood;
think of two great armies coming together
on a dusty field: when all the tumult ends,
there are some men who clatter off rejoicing,
    and others who stay;
these are all noble subjects for reflection,
but when you read my book, think of making love
late in the morning to a supple woman
    on a narrow bed.

IX

*   *   *   *   *   *
*   *   *   *   *   *
*   *   *   *   *   *

    wretched without you.
oh, I exaggerate.   exaggeration
flutters, poor timid gelding!   understatement

roars like a lion—and that imposing team
    draws my chariot
around the track unevenly   *   *
*   *   *   *   I wobble
*   *   *   *   *   *
    mistress of revels!

X

Another man, another woman lying
*   *   *   *   *   *
*   *   if it is my pleasure
    simply to watch you
*   *   *   *   *   *
*   *   and the laughter surrounding
the edges of our conversation, which
    silence devours.

XI

    (a)

but *you* will not escape from my embraces

    (b)

*   *   *   *   *   *
*   *   *   *   *   *
this also pleases her, delights the golden
    Venus of Eryx.

Note: Gaius Licinius Macer Calvus, 82–47 B.C. One of the closest friends of
Catullus, "he was renowned as a most able and skillful orator, though of low
stature, and as a writer of epic, lyric, and epigram" (Merrill). Only a few
fragments of his verse survive.

IV

Sharks at the New York Aquarium

Suddenly drawn through the thick glass plate
And swimming among them, I imagine
Myself as, briefly, part of the pattern
Traced in the water as they circulate
Endlessly, obeying the few laws
That thread the needle of their simple lives:
One moment in a window of serrated knives,
Old-fashioned razors and electric saws.
And then the sudden, steep, sidewinding pass:
No sound at all. The waters turning pink,
Then rose, then red, after a long while clear.
And here I am again, outside the tank,
Uneasily wrapped in our atmosphere!
Children almost never tap on the glass.

Finding Your Marbles

Once they were models of spherical clarity,
Bright, umblemished balls asleep in crystalline silence,
Cats' eyes glowing with sullen, inflexible colors.
Awakened, they clicked together smartly in their cigar box
And gave no trouble. But one by one they left you,
Scattering for the frayed edges of your attention
Until you forgot about them altogether.
Now they have all rolled back from wherever it was
That they were for such a long time: grooved and pitted
Almost beyond recognition, they manifest
No room at all between a rock and a hard place.
Your admiration for what they have gone through is pointless:
"Experience abrades, reveals *such* character. . . ."
—But it's a character which your experience
Hasn't a hope of ever understanding!
You were mistaken: these are no longer your marbles.

Museum Pieces

Too quick to admire
What we are easily bored by,
We drift along from case to case
Taking in the graceful

Penmanship of lost
Curators, men who trusted
The clear virtues of precise description.
Dead, they found heaven

A mansion full of halls
Like this one: along the walls
Were case after case of their own bones
(Each dyed with the blue stain

Of resurrection) newly
Arranged for them in mute
Tableaux by One who *did*, as it happened,
Believe in evolution. . . .

Or so we imagine.
Easier to entertain
Such fantasies than to pretend
To believe in the mending

Of bones that had been broken
For so long. Here they are whole
Again, and not at all convincing,
Despite the evidence

Of our senses, despite
The meatless hulk of frightful
Tyrannosaurus, majestic on his island's
Prow, scowling in abstract

Fury—the upraised king
We've come to see. Seeing,
In this case though, isn't believing.
These monsters are unreal

To us, elaborate
Fictions as second-rate
As the huge statue of T. R. on horseback,
Between the red and the black—

It's all very clever,
But nothing like them ever
Walked the earth. We refuse to believe it:
We have been put on, deceived

By expert forgers of bone
And bronze. Out of the ruin
Of one empire or another, they'll raise
A monument which praises

Things as they were not:
All of the terror forgotten,
All accidents simply not let to occur. . . .
A closet anarchist,

My reconstruction would
Restore all to rubble
Without meaning: nothing remaining
After the tuneless din

Of the "Mad" Concerto
For Cretaceous Xylophone
But a great lot of pieces scattered
On the floor. Or even better,

Only the empty hall
With no bones at all;
And begin over. Where there is room for error,
There is room for us.

59

Proposal for a Monument of Pears

Four pears in all, and all of them gigantic:
Two in the foreground looming up, obscurely
Questioning our values, giving answers
In an ambiguous fashion which will surely
Offer much comfort, solace: the distressed of
Heart will remain here in grey droves for hours,
Until the third pear seems to them the breast of
A green girl, ripening: beyond it towers
The patriarch of pears—orgulous, sullen,
Not to be sliced compliantly in wedges
And taken as dessert with runny cheeses:
Restored, the pilgrims sink upon their knees as
They see the carved words, brown around the edges,
Of its simple inscription: FOR THE FALLEN

Snapshot of Dracula

Where the face should be, with the thin white lips
Fixed in a smile from which wild honey drips,
There's nothing at all: the mask of assurance slips

From the face of the girl we see up there on the screen
Holding the snapshot carefully between
Two trembling fingers. She stares at the unseen,

The photographic image of non-Being
Beside the image of the image that we're seeing.
For a brief moment, she considers fleeing,

But he's right behind her, just as large as life
Can be, in the movies. And now we hear him laugh:
He too is staring at the photograph,

No doubt amused by this new development.
—How easily her young and impudent
Boyfriend, the Doctor from the States, was sent

Off on a wild goose chase to the crags
With Mumm the Hunchback, whose left leg drags
Behind him as he leads astray!
                              The girl sags,

The Count supports her. So little time to gloat,
So little time to tease that pulsing throat
Before the ending we have learned by rote:

The door flung open, and the poor Count, even
In the moment of his triumph, apprehended,
And the sharp stake driven,
Whuck, whuck, whuck. That Evil may be ended.

Poem in Brooklyn

Racket of buses
On Eighth Avenue:
You are out again
On the street as always
At nightfall, dark
Old woman—you
Who are such a great scandal!
—Muttering in Spanish,

But eager to learn
The flutings of another
Tongue, as though by staring
Up into the bright
Unblinded windows
Filled with expensive,
Fashionable green:
Diligent translator,

Rapt in your translation!
Each room you search
Must be completed
In your imagination,
Where every naked
Arm will find its shoulder
And each breast barely
Sighted be mated;

Thus we are all improved:
Those who were broken
Are once more made whole

By your nocturnal
Watches, your passionate care;
And those who live alone
Now have their great good friends
To keep them company.

No hypocrite voyeur,
You bob and weave
Behind parked cars,
Ma semblable, ma soeur,
Openly angling
For what we almost never
Get in this city:
The perfect view.

Love in the City of Light Bent Back

Being deceives, they believe: their existence
Depends on hours spent in front of the mirrors
Surrounding them. They watch as their reflections
Undress, dress and undress; they finger themselves
Coyly, with what they think of as abandon:
Though there is no one there who doesn't notice,

It is considered impolite to notice,
At least in public places, the existence
Of habits some deplore but none abandon;
No matter how far removed they are from mirrors
They must inevitably find themselves
As much involved with them as those reflections

Which are the subject of their best reflections:
"And how long will it be before they notice
That we can love only the images themselves,
And by so doing, have given them existence,
Have made them independent of the mirrors
Which they will certainly, in time, abandon?

"Were we to go so far as to abandon
This city which we love to its reflections,
Or forge a great hammer and shatter all the mirrors,
Those saucy images would not take notice;
How long before they question our existence?"
And even as the speakers reveal themselves

In troubled words, the very words themselves
Betray their speakers, rapidly abandon

Meaning and motive both: fade from existence
Like lovers stripped before their own reflections,
To echo in infinity unnoticed.
"Mere words," their saying goes, "will fog no mirrors."

That city, so unlike ours, strangely mirrors
Ours in some ways—ways which in themselves
May not matter. But of course you will notice
An explanation much too neat to abandon:
The people of that city are our reflections.
They say that it will pass out of existence

When the mirrors waken to their own existence:
Conscious of themselves, they will, without notice
Shatter, abandoning their lost reflections.

Taken Up

Tired of earth, they dwindled on their hill,
Watching and waiting in the moonlight until
The aspens' leaves quite suddenly grew still,

No longer quaking as the disc descended,
That glowing wheel of lights whose coming ended
All waiting and watching. When it landed

The ones within it one by one came forth,
Stalking out awkwardly upon the earth,
And those who watched them were confirmed in faith:

Mysterious voyagers from outer space,
Attenuated, golden—shreds of lace
Spun into seeds of the sunflower's spinning face—

Light was their speech, spanning mind to mind:
We come here not believing what we find—
Can it be your desire to leave behind

The earth, which even those called angels bless,
Exchanging amplitude for emptiness?
And in a single voice they answered *Yes*,

Discord of human melodies all bent
To the unearthly strain of their assent.
Come then, the Strangers said, and those who were taken went.